PARIS 2024 ULTIMATE TRAVEL GUIDE TO THE CITY OF LIGHT AND THE OLYMPICS

DISCOVER THE BEST OF PARIS FROM IT'S ICONIC LANDMARKS TO ITS HIDDEN GEMS TO PLAN YOUR TRIP TO THE 2024 OLYMPIC GAMES IN PARIS

ASHLEY M. TUCK

CONTENTS

CHAPTER 1

INTRODUCTION

Greetings, esteemed reader, and welcome to this captivating tome. I'm overjoyed that you've chosen to embark on this extraordinary odyssey with me. I am known as Ashley, a wanderer of the world and an ardent admirer of the enchanting metropolis of Paris. Countless times have I ventured to this bewitching city, unearthing countless novelties and wonders. Yet, a revelation awaits in the year 2024, as Paris prepares to unveil something truly extraordinary: the Olympic Games.

The grandeur of the Olympic Games is unparalleled, drawing together multitudes of athletes hailing from over 200 nations, competing in a myriad of disciplines. These Games embody an exultant tribute to human brilliance, diversity, and solidarity while acting as a catalyst for positive metamorphosis and advancement.

Paris 2024 shall mark the French capital's third occasion as host of the Olympic Games, following the inaugural events of 1900 and the resplendent Games of 1924. A milestone not to be missed, it shall also inaugurate Paris's premiere staging of the Paralympic Games. The Parisian canvas will unfurl its wonders, presenting a vivid panorama of iconic landmarks juxtaposed with hidden gems, and its timeless allure blended with contemporary innovation.

Allow me to unveil the reasons I deem Paris an irresistible siren beckoning your presence during the 2024 Olympic Games:

-Embrace an Unrivaled Theatrical Spectacle: Immerse yourself in an epoch-making celebration of athletic prowess, as the world's finest competitors vie for glory in a kaleidoscope of sports. Discover new passions, cheer for your homeland, or extend camaraderie to distant nations, and savor the thrilling emotion woven into each contest. Beyond the arenas, an array of cultural and educational events shall enrapture your senses, including exhibitions, concerts, festivals, and workshops.

- Embark on a Paradigm of Olympism: Paris 2024 shall unveil an epoch of Olympism brimming with freshness and ingenuity, characterized by inclusivity and sustainability. Novel sports like breakdancing, skateboarding, surfing, and sport climbing shall make their grand debut. This magnificent festivity shall span across France, even reaching the shores of Tahiti. With 95% reliance on existing or temporary venues, Paris shall bestow an enduring legacy upon the city and the nation.

- Immerse in One of Earth's Most Breathtaking Enclaves: Paris awaits to mesmerize every soul. Behold its resplendent architecture, like the majestic Louvre, the breathtaking Eiffel Tower, the venerable regal Arc de Triomphe, & Notre Dame. Traverse world-renowned museums like the Musée d'Orsay, the Pompidou Center, and the Orangerie. Wander through the labyrinthine streets of Montmartre, the Latin Quarter, and Canal Saint-Martin. Indulge your palate in exquisite cuisine, from buttery croissants to sumptuous wine and cheese. Experience a vivacious nightlife enveloping jazz clubs, cabarets, bars, and clubs.

- Relish Seamless and Effortless Travel: Among the globe's most accessible cities, Paris welcomes you with open arms. Arrive by air, rail, bus, or car, tailored to your preferences and locale. With three major airports—Charles de Gaulle (CDG), Orly (ORY), and Beauvais (BVA)—options abound. High-speed trains (TGV) whisk travelers from European cities to Paris's six principal train stations, including Gare du Nord and Gare de Lyon. Once in Paris, navigate with ease, courtesy of the comprehensive community conveyance system encompassing RER, metro, buses, trains, or bikes.

- Craft Timeless Memories with Loved Ones: Journeying to the city of light for the 2024 Olympic Games presents an unparalleled opportunity to craft indelible memories with cherished friends & family. Tailor your itinerary to passions and preferences, with an abundant array of activities and attractions at your disposal. Find accommodations suiting diverse budgets and requirements, from hotels and hostels to apartments and homestays. Avail yourself of numerous offers and discounts available exclusively to the esteemed visitors of this grand sporting spectacle.

Within the pages of this volume lies a treasure trove of insights to maximize your sojourn in Paris for the 2024 Olympic Games. It unfurls a wealth of practical information, guiding your passage to Paris, selecting the finest lodgings, pinpointing the must-see and do, acquiring event tickets, assimilating the city's rich culture and lifestyle, and much more.

Each chapter shall illuminate a unique facet of your pilgrimage. My heartfelt hope is that this manuscript serves as a wellspring of inspiration, urging you to partake in Paris's rapturous embrace during the 2024 Olympic Games, and thus ensuring an unforgettable escapade awaits. Like me, you, too, shall succumb to the city's inexorable charm. Let us embark on this extraordinary adventure!

CHAPTER 2

THE IN & OUT OF PARIS

Life is not about
finding yourself.
Life is about
creating yourself

How to get to Paris by plane, train, bus, or car

Embark on a journey to the captivating city of Paris, where avenues of possibilities await you. Arriving there is a breeze, and you have an array of choices tailored to your preferences and point of departure. In this exciting chapter, I'll be your guide, revealing the finest avenues to Paris by plane, train, bus, or car, while imparting wisdom on securing unbeatable deals and steering clear of swindles.

Flying, with its swiftness and convenience, stands as the premier option, particularly if you venture from distant lands. Behold Paris' trio of major airports: Charles de Gaulle (CDG), Orly (ORY), and Beauvais (BVA), each with its distinctive allure and drawbacks, depending on your destination, budget, and itinerary.

Charles de Gaulle Airport, a bustling colossus, reigns as Paris' foremost aviation gateway, situated 25 km (16 miles) northeast of the city center. Air France and other international airlines converge at this bustling hub, facilitating seamless connections from the U.S., Canada, Australia, and various corners of Europe. With an array of trans-Atlantic airlines gracing its runways, including the likes of Norwegian, American Airlines, Air France, Air Canada, and Emirates, CDG serves as the nexus of global travel.

Once you find yourself landing on CDG's welcoming tarmac, Paris' radiant heart beckons. Swoop into the city center through a myriad of options:

- Take the RER's line B, whisking you away to various central stations. A ticket costing €10.30 (US$ 11.60) ushers you on a 35-minute adventure.

- Embrace the charm of the bus, as various lines crisscross the city, offering access to diverse neighborhoods. Fares ranging from €6 (US$ 6.80) to €17 (US$ 19.20) reveal an affordable and picturesque journey of 45 to 90 minutes.

- Hail a taxi at the station exit or secure a reservation online for a swift and seamless passage to your destination. With fixed fares of €50 (US$ 56.50) for the right bank of the Seine and €55 (US$ 62) for the left bank, your voyage typically takes 30 to 60 minutes, though whimsical traffic might sway the duration.

- In the modern age of ride-hailing, Uber stands ready to whisk you to Paris' heart with comfort and ease. Expect fares ranging from €35 (US$ 39.50) to €60 (US$ 67.80), adapting to the ebb and flow of demand and the time of day. Delight in a 30 to 60-minute sojourn, accompanied by the mesmerizing views of Parisian streets.

Orly Airport, its splendor second to none, lies 13 km (8 miles) south of Paris' core, serving as a gateway for domestic and European flights. Welcoming those from various European cities and North Africa, Orly extends a warm reception to travelers. With an assortment of airlines, including Vueling, Easyjet, Transavia, and Air France, ORY casts a spell of wanderlust upon all who arrive.

As you alight at Orly, prepare for an enchanting voyage to the heart of Paris through a medley of options:

- The RER's line B once again emerges as a reliable path, propelling you to various central stations in a 40-minute journey. Secure a ticket for €12.10 (US$ 13.70) either at the station or through online portals.

- Climb aboard the bus and relish the tapestry of the cityscape en route to diverse destinations. Fares ranging from €1.90 (US$ 2.10) to €12 (US$ 13.60) grant you passage for 30 to 60 minutes, embracing the rhythm of Parisian life.

- Surrender to the allure of a taxi, beckoning at the station exit or booked in advance. Fixed fares of €35 (US$ 39.50) for the left bank and €30 (US$ 33.90) for the right bank whisk you away for a 20 to 40-minute escapade through the city's arteries.

- In the digital age, Uber stands as a faithful companion, ready to fulfill your Parisian dreams. Fare estimates, ranging from €20 (US$ 22.60) to €40 (US$ 45.20), cater to the whims of demand and time, ensuring a 20 to 40-minute odyssey through Paris' enchanting embrace.

Beauvais Airport (BVA), is a petite gem tucked 85 km (53 miles) to the north of Paris's vibrant heart. This delightful airstrip primarily caters to budget-savvy adventurers, offering a gateway to some splendid European cities. Picture yourself soaring from Dublin, Rome Ciampino, or Barcelona El Prat with the likes of Ryanair, while Wizz Air whisks you away from Budapest Ferenc Liszt, Warsaw Chopin, or Sofia. And let's not forget Blue Air's enchanting routes from Bucharest Henri Coandă, Cluj-Napoca Avram Iancu, and Iași.

Now, suppose you've landed at BVA, eager to explore the City of Lights. Fear not! There's a nifty bus option awaiting you. A charming shuttle bus stands ready to whisk you from BVA to Porte Maillot in the heart of Paris. Surrender a mere €17 (US$ 19.20), and in just 75 magical minutes, you'll find yourself immersed in the enchanting streets of this captivating city.

Yet, if you hail from more distant European realms, allow me to unveil the wonders of Paris's six majestic train stations: Gare du Nord, Gare de l'Est, Gare de Lyon, Gare d'Austerlitz, Gare Montparnasse, and Gare Saint-Lazare. Each is a portal to a different corner of France and Europe, where high-speed trains (TGV), regional trains (TER), and international trains (Eurostar, Thalys, and more) eagerly await to whisk you away on grand adventures.

Imagine the thrill of reaching London via the illustrious Eurostar, embracing the hustle of Brussels in the Thalys' embrace, or savoring Amsterdam's delights, all from the beating heart of Gare du Nord.

Hear the whispers of Cologne's history while nestled in the Thalys carriage, or feel the rhythm of Strasbourg's heartbeat from Gare de l'Est. The scenic charm of Frankfurt awaits you in just under four magical hours. Or dare to venture to Berlin aboard the ICE on a journey that will etch unforgettable memories for eight hours and nine minutes.

To make your escapade seamless, avail yourself of ingenious train search engines like Trainline or Omio, guiding you to the perfect ticket, all at your fingertips.

Once you arrive at the stations, the splendor of Paris's public transport unfolds before you. Hop on the sleek metro lines and traverse the city's veins, venturing from station to station with a mere €1.90 (US$ 2.10) in hand. The RER is another magical option, whisking you to Parisian hotspots with equal charm and speed.

Oh, but should you fancy the scenic route, embark on a delightful bus ride through Paris's streets. For just €2 (US$ 2.30), let the city's rhythm take you to hidden corners and vibrant boulevards.

Now, for those seeking comfort and convenience, a majestic taxi awaits at the station's doorstep. Allow an official taxi to usher you into the heart of Paris, where the fare dances playfully between €10 (US$ 11.30) and €20 (US$ 22.60), depending on the route and the whims of traffic.

And lastly, we have the modern chariot, Uber. Tap your way to a splendid journey through the Uber app, where the fare's fluctuating dance ranges from €8 (US$ 9) to €15 (US$ 16.90), all while gliding through Paris's picturesque roads.

If your purse strings are feeling tight or you crave a last-minute escapade, let the wheels of a bus transport you to the City of Lights. Paris boasts numerous bus stations, each serving as a gateway to various regions in France and beyond Porte Maillot, Bercy Seine, Gallieni, and La Défense.

Fear not the cost, for a plethora of modern coaches await your arrival at these stations, from the likes of Flixbus, and Ouibus, to Eurolines, and more. Fancy a rendezvous with London in a mere 9 hours? Catch the Flixbus departing from Porte Maillot. Brussels beckons from the same station, a mere 4-hour affair. And if Amsterdam's allure beckons, hop on a Flixbus for a 6-hour sojourn. Venture deeper into Europe with Flixbus, meandering through the charm of Cologne in 7 hours or embracing Berlin's vibrant spirit in a 14-hour odyssey from Bercy Seine. Oui, Ouibus caters to your whims as well, whisking you to Lyon, Marseille, or even sunny Barcelona.

But worry not, dear traveler, for once you arrive at these bus stations, Paris unfurls its avenues to your eager feet. Choose from a metro adventure, where you'll weave through the underground, savoring the city's heartbeat in a brisk 10 to 20 minutes. Fancy the RER? Traverse its veins and emerge in the heart of Paris, your journey just as swift and soul-stirring.

Opt for a bus ride through Paris's streets, the city unfurling its secrets as you meander along its boulevards. Expect a leisurely 15 to 30 minutes, depending on traffic's caprice. Should you crave the swift embrace of a taxi, they await, perched by the station's exit or a mere app tap away. But if modern technology enchants you, summon an Uber to whisk you away, the city's magic unfurling through the window as you glide toward your destination.

Still, some choose to embrace the road less traveled and seek the freedom of driving to Paris. The highways and roads sing with promise, connecting you to distant regions of France and Europe. But beware, oh daring souls, for Parisian roads come with a price – challenges aplenty, traffic's tempest, tolls, parking woes, and the watchful eye of environmental restrictions.

As you venture from distant lands to join this cosmopolitan dance, ensure your documents are in order – a valid license, international driving permit, car registration, insurance, and identification in hand. Fear not the mandatory Crit'Air sticker; it's but a token to embrace this city's ecological ideals.

Embark from London, tracing the M20, tunneling through Folkestone, and soaring on Eurotunnel's wings. You'll savor the journey for about 6 hours, with the crossing time a tale in itself. From Brussels, the A8 and E19 shall guide your path, Paris's embrace reached in a mere 3-hour embrace.

As you drive from Amsterdam, the A2 and A27 weave a tale, leading to Utrecht's enchantment. The A12 and E25 weave your path to Antwerp, with the E19 guiding you to Lille's arms. Then, the A1 beckons you to Paris, the whole escapade gifting you a 5-hour adventure.

Cologne's allure is yours to savor, tracing the A4 to Aachen, E40 to Liège, E42 to Namur, and E411 to Luxembourg. The A3 and A31 usher you to Metz, and finally, the A4 bears you to Paris, this journey spanning about 5 hours.

From Strasbourg, follow the A4, and after a 4-hour embrace, Paris's embrace awaits. Frankfurt's spirit calls, leading you along the A3, Cologne's allure mirrored in your path, and the rest mirrors your journey from Cologne.

Oh, Berlin, distant and yet so near, your path takes you along the A2 to Hannover and A7 to Kassel. The A5, A4, and the rest will be your guiding stars, as you journey for about 10 hours to Paris's embrace.

From Lyon, the A6 leads you straight to Paris, your journey a swift 4-hour symphony. And if Marseille beckons embrace the A7, and the journey mirrors your Lyon adventure.

CHAPTER 3

FINDING ACCOMMODATION IN PARIS

Unlocking the Perfect Parisian Abode:

Your Spirited Sojourn through Enchanting Arrondissements

Ah, the mesmerizing metropolis of Paris! A pulsating region that caters to all souls, though the task of settling on the ideal neighborhood can prove quite the adventure, particularly for the uninitiated. Fear not, intrepid traveler, for Paris unfurls like a captivating thread woven into twenty charismatic districts, known as arrondissements, spiraling from the core to the city's fringes. Each district weaves its distinct character, allure, and allurements, diverging wildly in cost, ambiance, and convenience.

Join me on this daring expedition, and together, we shall unearth the finest area to lay your hat in Paris, tailored to your whims, fancies, and financial flair.

Beyond this, behold, as I reveal the most magnetic neighborhoods replete with glamor and intrigue. As for your home-away-from-home, fear not, for I shall recommend the finest boutique hotels and pieds-à-terre in each locale, ensuring a sojourn unlike any other.

The Grand Rendezvous for Paris' first-timers: Louvre/Tuileries, 1st arrondissement

Seeking proximity to Paris' paramount treasures such as the illustrious Louvre Museum, the resplendent Tuileries Garden, the illustrious Place de la Concorde, and the legendary Champs-Élysées? The 1st arrondissement awaits, the beating heart of Paris itself, boasting architectural wonders, a treasury of culture, and an ancient history to savor. Not to mention, it's an ideal locale for indulging in the city's premier shopping, gastronomy, and nightlife. Fear not the urban web, as excellent public transit options abound, whisking you away to distant districts and fairytale day trips to Versailles or Disneyland.

A word of caution, dear traveler, this sought-after domain teems with tourists and opulence, perhaps sacrificing tranquility and authenticity in favor of unbridled exuberance and bustle. Nevertheless, brace yourself to be enchanted!

Now, allow me to present the creme de la creme of lodgings in this coveted region:

- Hotel Regina Louvre: A lavish 5-star haven, boasting regal chambers and suites, bestowing breathtaking vistas of the Louvre and the Eiffel Tower. Here, dine in grandeur, sip at the bar, and hone your physique at the fitness center, all while the impeccable concierge service caters to your every whim.

- Hotel du Louvre: A chic 4-star treasure, adorned with tasteful chambers and suites, each an ode to artistry inspired by the Louvre Museum. Savor culinary delights at the in-house restaurant, savor libations at the bar, and allow the 24-hour front desk to weave seamless perfection into your stay.

- Hotel Crayon by Elegancia: A whimsical 3-star hideaway, with vivacious rooms and suites, replete with modern amenities and vibrant touches. Find solace in the lounge, enjoy a delightful breakfast, and bask in the warm embrace of the amiable staff.

- Louvre Palais Royal Apartments: A collection of palatial apartments, offering commodious living spaces, fully-equipped kitchens, and charming balconies overlooking the Louvre Museum and the Palais Royal Gardens. Discover the joy of residing like a Parisian monarch!

For the Food Explorer: Les Halles, 1st & 2nd arrondissement

Is your heart attuned to the delectable symphony of French cuisine? Look no further than Les Halles, the epicurean epicenter, once the very heartbeat of Parisian markets. Although the historic central market may have given way to the modern splendor of Forum des Halles, the spirit of gastronomy still thrives, with a cornucopia of restaurants, bistros, bakeries, and specialty shops to tempt your taste buds.

Herein lies a world of flavors—classic French delicacies, international culinary wonders, street food extravaganzas, and high-end indulgences. Traverse the enchanting Rue Montorgueil, a pedestrian boulevard adorned with food stalls, markets, and terraces, where each step unveils a new delight. And fear not, fellow foodie, for besides sating your appetite, this vibrant domain boasts the Pompidou Center, the revered Saint-Eustache Church, and the stately Palais Royal—ample culture and nightlife to satiate all cravings!

A word to the wise, though, this vivacious hub thrives in full clamor and hustle, a sensory whirlwind worth every moment, but brace for the occasional urban tempest.

Now, allow me to tantalize your taste buds with a selection of lodgings in this culinary haven:

- Hotel Bachaumont: A trendy 4-star oasis, where sleek chambers and suites bless you with panoramic city views and well-stocked minibars. Wine and dine at the restaurant, unwind at the bar, sculpt your body at the fitness center, and trust the 24-hour front desk to whisk away any cares.

- Hotel Snob by Elegancia: A stylish 3-star gem, boasting cozy chambers and suites, adorned in vintage elegance and modern comfort. Greet the day with breakfast delights, relax in the lounge, and bask in the care of the thoughtful concierge.

- Hotel des Halles: A charming 2-star haven, where simplicity is the essence of bliss. Enjoy free Wi-Fi and air conditioning, savor breakfast delights, and savor the warmth of the attentive staff.

- Les Halles Apartments: A gallery of capacious and sumptuous apartments, each graced with fully-equipped kitchens, living spaces designed for leisure, and delightful balconies to take in the surrounding allure. Nestled close to Forum des Halles and Rue Montorgueil, this is the pinnacle of gastronomic lodging.

For the Fashionista'sChamps-Élysées/Golden Triangle, 8th arrondissement

Calling all style mavens! Prepare to immerse yourself in the chicest domain of Paris, the 8th arrondissement, where shopaholic dreams come true. Embrace the dazzling allure of the Champs-Élysées, a legendary avenue adorned with opulent boutiques, flagship stores, and swanky eateries. And that's not all; dare to explore the Golden Triangle, the glitzy enclave nestled between Champs-Élysées, Avenue Montaigne, and Avenue George V, where the crème de la crème of fashion houses await – Dior, Chanel, Louis Vuitton, Givenchy, and more.

The 8th arrondissement exudes sophistication, an upscale sanctuary teeming with iconic landmarks like the regal Arc de Triomphe, the magnificent Grand Palais, the Petit Palais, and the stately Place de la Concorde. Gaze in awe at breathtaking vistas of the Eiffel Tower and the Seine River, making every moment an Instagram-worthy masterpiece.

Yet, be forewarned, dear fashionistas; this alluring paradise of couture and charm comes with a hefty price tag and throngs of tourists. Brace yourself for the glamorous whirlwind and pulsating energy that envelops this fashion mecca.

Embark on a fabulous sojourn, residing in some of the most luxurious hotels and apartments this realm has to offer:

- Hotel Barrière Le Fouquet's: A palatial 5-star oasis, where sumptuous rooms and suites boast balconies, presenting vistas of Champs-Élysées or the majestic Eiffel Tower. Indulge in pampering at the opulent spa, take a dip in the pool, sculpt your body at the fitness center, savor culinary delights at the restaurant, sip cocktails at the bar, and let the attentive concierge cater to your every whim.

- Hotel Vernet: A sophisticated 4-star haven, where elegant rooms and suites feature marble bathrooms and well-stocked minibars. Revel in delectable dishes at the restaurant, unwind in style at the bar, stay active at the fitness center, and trust the 24-hour front desk to attend to your desires.

- Hotel Elysées Céramic: A vibrant 3-star gem, with quirky rooms and suites, adorned with free Wi-Fi and air conditioning. Delight in a breakfast feast, bask in the ambiance of the terrace and bask in the warmth of the friendly staff.

- Champs Elysees Apartments: A selection of lavish and expensive apartments, each flaunting fully equipped kitchens, living areas designed for ultimate comfort, and private balconies, all conveniently located near Champs-Élysées and the iconic Arc de Triomphe.

Saint-Germain-des-Prés,6th arrondissement-A Parisian Playground for Families

Embarking on a family adventure?

Look no further than the captivating embrace of Saint-Germain-des-Prés, an enchanting and historical neighborhood in the heart of Paris, radiating with artistic flair and literary charm. Here, beauty beckons at every corner, from picturesque architecture to cozy cafés and quaint bookshops.

Unearth treasures at some of the city's finest museums and galleries – Musée d'Orsay, Musée Rodin, and Musée du Luxembourg, all waiting to enthrall young minds and curious souls alike. Rejoice, for Saint-Germain-des-Prés is a family-friendly haven, teeming with verdant parks, playgrounds, and a plethora of kid-friendly activities. Stroll along the Seine River, marvel at the grandeur of Notre Dame Cathedral, explore the vibrant Latin Quarter, or embark on a magical boat ride aboard the Bateaux-Mouches. The neighborhood also boasts a plethora of restaurants, bakeries, and ice cream parlors catering to the whims of young ones. But heed this advice, dear families: popularity comes at a price. Plan, for this cherished locale tends to attract both tourists and higher prices, especially during peak seasons.

Let me unveil a selection of splendid hotels and apartments, sure to weave unforgettable family memories:

- Hotel Lutetia: A grand 5-star retreat, with spacious rooms and suites offering dazzling views of the Eiffel Tower or the serene Seine River. Indulge in relaxation at the splendid spa, take a dip in the pool, stay active at the fitness center, savor delectable cuisine at the restaurant, sip cocktails at the bar, and entrust the concierge with your every wish.

- Hotel Bel Ami: A modern 4-star gem, where bright rooms and suites are equipped with free Wi-Fi and air conditioning. Revel in rejuvenation at the serene spa, stay fit at the fitness center, relish fine dining at the restaurant, unwind at the bar, and count on the 24-hour front desk for seamless experiences.

- Hotel de Nesle: A quirky 3-star haven, with uniquely themed rooms and suites, complete with free Wi-Fi. Delight in the garden, bask in the ambiance of the lounge area and cherish the care of the friendly staff.

- Saint Germain Apartments: A haven of expansive apartments, brimming with creature comforts, fully equipped kitchens, living spaces inviting relaxation, and charming balconies. Conveniently located near the Saint-Germain-des-Prés Church and the Boulevard Saint-Germain, these lodgings ensure family bliss.

Uncover the Enchanting Village Vibes:

Montmartre, 18th arrondissement

Yearning to embrace the true essence of Parisian bohemia? Look no further than the charismatic realm of Montmartre, where authenticity thrives and artistic souls find solace. Ascend the famed hilltop to behold the majestic Sacré-Cœur Basilica, meander through the lively Place du Tertre, and wander the quaint cobblestone streets and staircases. Here, you'll unravel the rich artistic heritage of Montmartre, where visionaries like Picasso, Renoir, and Dalí once roamed, and where legendary cabarets like the Moulin Rouge and the Lapin Agile captivated the masses.

Indulge in picturesque romance, as stunning city vistas unfold before your eyes, while intimate bistros and cafés beckon with delectable delights. Seek out secret gardens and hidden vineyards, embracing the poetic charm that infuses every corner. And as night falls, immerse yourself in the vibrant nightlife, where shopping, entertainment, and a kaleidoscope of experiences await.

Yet, heed the traveler's wisdom; this treasured paradise exudes allure, drawing crowds and tourists to its very heart. Prepare for steep ascents, stairs, and uneven paths, as the price for enchantment is sometimes paid in delightful challenges.

Lose Yourself in the Heart of Fashion and Nightlife: The Marais, 3rd & 4th Arrondissements

Seeking an urban playground where trends converge, galleries inspire, and the night pulses with life? Say no more – the Marais stands as Paris' epicenter of culture and style, a realm of historic grandeur interwoven with avant-garde flair. Traverse its streets, where chic boutiques, eclectic galleries, and delightful bistros beckon your curiosity. Find yourself captivated by the vibrant artistry that breathes life into every corner, from the Musée Picasso to the Musée Carnavalet and beyond. And don't forget to wander through the captivating Place des Vosges, a living testament to elegance and history.

But the allure of the Marais doesn't end with art and culture; this is a district that embraces diversity and inclusion, boasting a mosaic of cultural influences. Journey through the Jewish Quarter, bask in the vivacity of the Gay Village and savor the richness of Chinatown. And let's not forget the dynamic street art, vibrant markets, and the pulsating energy of festive celebrations that weave through this spirited haven.

Be warned, though, as with all things trendy, the Marais is a whirlwind of activity, bustling and alive, especially on weekends and evenings. Prepare for narrow passageways, traffic jams, and charming chaos that dances in rhythm with the city's heartbeat.

Prepare for an Extraordinary Sojourn:

- Hotel du Petit Moulin: A 4-star gem exuding chic style, where elegant rooms and suites, graced with free Wi-Fi and air conditioning, invite comfort and relaxation. Revel in luxury at the spa, stay fit at the fitness center, savor culinary delights at the restaurant, and let the concierge curate your every desire.

- Hotel Jules & Jim: A 3-star haven of trendiness, with minimalist rooms and suites offering free Wi-Fi and air conditioning. Begin your day with a delectable breakfast, unwind in the enchanting courtyard, sip cocktails at the bar, and count on the 24-hour front desk for seamless experiences.

- Hotel de la Bretonnerie: A 2-star treasure of charm, with cozy rooms and suites boasting free Wi-Fi and air conditioning. Partake in delightful breakfast offerings, linger in the inviting lounge area, and relish the warm embrace of the friendly staff.

- Marais Apartments: A selection of splendid and spacious apartments, each equipped with fully-furnished kitchens, living rooms for relaxation, delightful dining areas, and captivating balconies. Discover the allure of residing near the Pompidou Center and the vibrant Rue des Rosiers.

Unlocking Your Dream Stay in Paris: Embrace the Adventure of Finding Your Perfect Accommodation!

With the allure of Paris, comes the financial challenges of finding your ideal abode. Fear not, for a plethora of options awaits you - hotels, hostels, Airbnbs, and Couchsurfing, each holding a treasure trove of experiences tailored to your preferences, budget, and expectations.

Join me on this quest to unearth the best hotel, hostel, Airbnb, or Couchsurfing in Paris, armed with savvy tips for booking in advance or embracing last-minute spontaneity, all while bagging the finest deals and discounts.

Embark on the Dance of Timing:

- Availability: Preplanning ensures a plethora of options, securing your dream location, amenities, and price, especially during peak seasons or grand events. Yet, flexibility may wane, limiting your ability to pivot or cancel plans. Embrace the thrill of the last-minute gambit, opening doors to spontaneity, but be prepared for fewer choices or premium prices. Compromises may beckon, yet that's the beauty of a daring adventure!

- Price: Early bird catches the worm, and booking in advance may reward you with lower prices or enticing early bird discounts. Equip yourself with powerful tools like Skyscanner or Kayak to scour comparison websites and apps, and let loyalty programs or rewards cards become your secret allies. However, latecomers, fear not, for last-minute deals may be your saving grace! Harness the might of websites or apps like HotelTonight or LastMinute, and wield the power of negotiation with hosts or owners. After all, you're in charge of your destiny!

- Quality: A well-prepared journey promises higher quality accommodation. Immerse yourself in the experiences of previous guests through reviews, ratings, and photos, and connect directly with hosts or owners to craft your ideal stay. Yet, take heed of the lurking shadows, for false advertising and hidden fees may lurk. Adventurers seeking spontaneity can thrive too! Rely on verified hosts and owners on platforms like HotelTonight, ensuring delightful surprises, not unwelcome ones.

Mastering the Art of Deals and Discounts:

- Platform Comparisons: The path to savings lies in the art of platform comparison. Peruse diverse platforms for your preferred type of accommodation. Hotels, hostels, Airbnbs, and Couchsurfing may each offer a treasure trove of offers and prices. Unearth the hidden gems of comparison websites like Booking.com or Expedia, hostel-specific havens like Hostelworld or Hostelbookers, or the realm of Airbnb itself. Choose wisely, and let your budget thrive!

- Embrace Coupons and Promo Codes: Questing for the ultimate deal? Venture forth into the realm of coupons and promo codes, seeking discounts and perks to elevate your stay. Fret not, for online seekers shall find salvation on websites like RetailMeNot or Honey, unlocking the secrets to savings. Follow the virtual whispers of newsletters and social media accounts, and uncover exclusive offers or codes - an adventurer's best weapon!

- Flexibility Brings Fortunes: Let go of rigidity, and a world of possibilities shall unfold before you. Embrace the magic of off-seasons and weekdays, for they might whisper of lower prices and grander deals. Venture beyond the well-trodden paths, and seek solace in less central or lesser-known areas. Yet, remain cautious, for convenience and safety must not be sacrificed at the altar of savings.

- The Power of Direct Booking: Venture forth with courage, and forge a direct path to hosts or owners themselves. Avoid the tolls of extra fees and commissions levied by third-party platforms, and unleash the power of negotiation. Let your charm and charisma sway them in your favor, and may discounts flow forth like a river of riches.

CHAPTER 4

ENJOYING THE OLYMPIC GAMES

The Paris 2024 Olympic Games are just around the corner, and it's time to get pumped for this epic sporting extravaganza. Whether you're planning to be in the heart of the action or joining in from the comfort of your couch, here's your ultimate guide to making the most out of this unforgettable experience.

1. Snagging Your Tickets:

It's all about securing your golden tickets to witness history in the making! Head over to the official Paris 2024 ticketing hub and dive into a treasure trove of options. From individual events to jam-packed packages, you're in control of your Olympic adventure. And here's a pro tip: whip out your Visa card – they're the official payment maestros of the Games!

Or, for true VIP treatment, explore those swanky hospitality packages. Picture this – exclusive guest areas, premium services, and rubbing shoulders with the who's who of sports – now that's how you do it in style!

2. Unleash the Olympic Games Online and on TV:

Can't make it to the City of Lights? Fret not! The digital world has your back! Tap into the streaming wonders of Peacock, Eurosport Player, CBC Gem, 7plus, and Discovery+ – your front-row seats to all the Olympic action. Embrace the binge-watching spirit and catch those events, live or on-demand.

If you're a good ol' television enthusiast, NBC, Eurosport, CBC, Seven Network, and Sony Pictures

Networks have got you covered. Kick back, relax, and let those epic moments unfold on the big screen!

Don't forget the social media frenzy! Facebook, Twitter, Instagram, YouTube, TikTok, Snapchat – they'll be your buzzing hubs for the juiciest news, updates, and behind-the-scenes stories from the Games. Talk about staying in the know, right?

3. Navigating the Spectacular Venues:

Now, let's get you oriented in this athletic wonderland. Grab the official Paris 2024 venue map – your treasure map to the Olympics! Discover the lowdown on location, capacity, accessibility, and all the electrifying events happening at each venue. Time to make your game plan!

Getting around is a breeze with the Paris 2024 transport map. Hop on the metro, bus, tram, or train, or go full-on eco-warrior and bike your way to the action. Just imagine cruising through Paris, the City of Love and Sports!

Oh, and a quick reminder – the devil is in the details. The official Paris 2024 ticketing website will dish out the 411 on parking, security, and all those essential services at each venue. No surprises, just smooth sailing!

Let the Games Begin!

It's finally here! The opening ceremony on Friday 26 July 2024, at 9 p.m. local time at the iconic Stade de France. Circle that date on your calendar – it's showtime, folks! The grand finale, the closing ceremony, will follow suit on Sunday 11 August 2024, at 9 p.m. local time, at the same rocking venue. Get your game face on!

Ace Your Ticket Hunt:

1. Claim Your Piece of History: Mark your spot at the opening and closing ceremonies by hitting up the official Paris 2024 ticketing website. Be an early bird – tickets vanish like lightning!

2. Ready, Set, Go!: Competition is fierce, but you're a champion! Be swift and have backup plans in your back pocket if Plan A doesn't pan out.

3. Lady Luck's Embrace: High-demand events may employ a lottery system – it's your chance to snatch

those elusive tickets! Play your cards right, and fortune might favor you.

4. Go Premium: If all else fails, seek out those premium tickets. A bit of extra sparkle might just elevate your experience to the stratosphere!

Cheer, Roar, and Celebrate:

This isn't just a sporting event; it's a global celebration of passion, unity, and excellence! Here's how you can bring your A-game to support your country and favorite athletes:

1. Colors of Pride: Drape yourself in your nation's colors, wave those flags, and show off your national flair with style!

2. Anthem of Unity: When the national anthem plays, raise your voice alongside fellow fans and athletes – a chorus of unity that'll send chills down your spine.

3. Make Some Noise: Let your energy explode! Clap, chant, and get the party started – be the life of the Olympic party!

4. Social Connect: Dive into the digital frenzy! Follow your team and athletes on social media, share the love, and create a global fan community.

5. Beyond the Cheers: Be a hero in your own right! Donate to support your country's athletes or lend a helping hand as a volunteer – you'll be a part of their journey to greatness.

This dazzling celebration brings together the crème de la crème of athletes from every corner of the globe, all set to compete in a jaw-dropping array of 32 sports and 329 events.

From the classics that have stood the test of time, like athletics, swimming, and gymnastics, to the trendy newcomers like breaking (the hip-hop dance phenomenon!), sport climbing, skateboarding, and surfing, this year's Olympics promise to be a captivating blend of tradition and innovation. These fresh and funky sports made their debut in Tokyo 2020 and have quickly become fan favorites, captivating the hearts of the youth and infusing the Games with creativity and zest.

Now, let me give you a sneak peek into the essence of some of the sports that will leave us breathless at the 2024 Olympics:

Archery - A sport that's as ancient as time itself! Picture this: skilled archers, armed with powerful bows, aiming at distant targets. Recurve and compound archery will take center stage, where archers will unleash their skills to hit the bull's eye and claim victory for their nations.

Athletics - The true embodiment of athleticism! This ultimate melting pot of speed, strength, endurance, and finesse will leave you in awe. The stadium will witness an array of dazzling track events, gravity-defying jumps, and Herculean throws, as athletes push the boundaries of human potential. Oh, and don't miss the thunderous sprints in the men's 100 meters dash, where history-making speedsters will leave a blazing trail on the track!

Badminton - Prepare for some lightning-fast racket action! Hailing from its origins in India and soaring high as a global sensation, badminton will showcase swift shuttlecock exchanges and exhilarating net play. Whether in electrifying singles or dynamic doubles matches, the badminton pros will captivate us with their lightning reflexes and tactical brilliance.

Basketball - A sport born from a stroke of genius! Take a trip back to 1891 when James Naismith dreamt up a game that now rules the hearts of millions. In the heart-pounding basketball tournaments, we'll witness five-player dream teams soaring through the air, slam-dunking their way to victory with epic hoop action!

Basketball 3x3 – the Olympic's newest gem! Picture this: three-player teams battling it out on a half-court, vying for that glorious slam-dunk into the hoop. With only 10 minutes on the clock or the first to reach 21 points, every second counts! The scoring system spices things up too, with one-point shots from inside the arc, two points from beyond the arc, and free throws all adding up to high-flying thrills! Brace yourselves for some intense showdowns in the men's and women's tournaments!

Now, let's step into the fierce realm of boxing. This ancient combat sport takes us back to its roots in 1904 when it joined the Olympic family. With two fighters donning gloves, the ring becomes a battleground where they exchange powerful punches. Each match has a set number of rounds or ends with a decisive knockout.

Weight classes add another layer of excitement, ensuring fair fights that'll keep us on the edge of our seats. Watch as the judges' scorecards or electrifying knockouts determine the victors in the 13 thrilling events!

And for those who seek the thrill of the wild waters, canoe slalom will leave you gasping for breath! Imagine navigating a canoe or kayak through gates on a wild whitewater river or artificial channel. The paddlers must skillfully maneuver their way through upstream and downstream gates, racing against time and receiving penalties for any slip-ups. The fastest, most precise paddler emerges as the conqueror in the four riveting events!

For those craving a dose of speed and stamina, canoe sprint and road cycling have got you covered! In canoe sprint, witness paddlers racing on calm waters over various distances, fiercely competing in lanes to reach that coveted finish line first. On the other hand, road cycling takes us back to the roots of the modern Olympics. We'll marvel at cyclists battling it out on paved roads, some racing against the clock in individual time trials, while others fight for position in mass start races. The thrilling action in these sports will leave us in awe!

Let's not forget the thrilling world of cycling track —
an oval-shaped track with steeply banked curves
where riders blaze through the air with speed and
finesse! With races ranging from sprints to endurance
events, the cycling track showcases the epitome of
cycling prowess. Keep an eye on the team sprint and
pursuit events, where strategies are as crucial as
speed in determining the winners. And of course, the
Omnium and Madison events, where riders compete
across a series of races, will keep us on our toes!

Also, for the daredevils among us, mountain biking
offers a wild ride through off-road trails and
obstacles! Since its debut in 1996, it has thrilled
audiences with cross-country races that push riders to
their limits. With breathtaking scenery and thrilling
obstacles, the men's and women's cross-country
events will leave us in awe of these fearless athletes!

Let's buckle up for the jaw-dropping stunts of BMX freestyle! These fearless riders will take on ramps, rails, and boxes, performing gravity-defying tricks that will leave us in awe. With one-minute runs on a course packed with obstacles, the event will be fierce! Judges will scrutinize their every move, scoring them based on difficulty, originality, style, flow, and execution. In the end, only the rider with the biggest score will claim victory in both the male and female park events!

Next, let's saddle up for an elegant event! Here, the bond between horse and rider takes center stage. Equestrian offers a trio of disciplines: dressage, eventing, and jumping. In the mesmerizing dressage category, the horse and rider will perform a graceful ballet of movements, harmonizing as one. Eventing will test their mettle across three days, with dressage, cross-country, and jumping, showcasing both finesse and bravery. Jumping, on the other hand, will see horses and riders tackling a course of obstacles with unparalleled speed and precision. In six captivating events, we'll witness the breathtaking synergy between these magnificent animals and their skilled riders!

Prepare for the clashing blades and lightning reflexes of fencing, the elegant combat sport! Fencers will wield three different weapons – foil, épée, and saber – engaging in electrifying duels where timing and strategy are everything. With electronic scoring systems, every touch will be counted, and the fencer with the most score at the stop of three minutes or the 1st to reach 15 points will ensure victory. In twelve occurrences for both sexes, the piste will be set ablaze with the pursuit of glory!

For those who crave the thrill of the beautiful tournament, football brings its enchanting magic to the city of light! The planet's most beloved sport will see teams of eleven players battling it out on the rectangular field, aiming to net that crucial goal. With skillful dribbles, precise passes, and breathtaking shots, these football stars will enthrall us throughout the tournaments!

Golf, another timeless classic, returns to Paris in 2024 after a long absence! We'll witness the finesse and precision of individual players as they navigate through a challenging 18-hole course. The player with the lowest score after four rounds will claim victory in both the men's and women's events!

Now, let's leap into the realm of gravity-defying acrobatics in artistic gymnastics! This high-flying sport combines strength, flexibility, and sheer artistry, as gymnasts showcase their skills on six apparatuses for men and four for women. With routines set to amaze and astonish, each performance will be scrutinized for difficulty, execution, and artistry. The gymnast or team with the highest total score will ascend to the podium in eight thrilling events for men and six for women!

Also, let's revel in the captivating elegance of rhythmic gymnastics! With their mesmerizing performances set to music, individual and group gymnasts will wield rope, hoop, ball, clubs, and ribbon with grace and precision. Judges will score them based on their breathtaking artistry, expression, and difficulty. Only those who flawlessly blend beauty and skill will triumph in both the individual all-around and group all-around events!

Trampoline! Picture this – gymnasts soaring through the air, executing mesmerizing flips and twists on a trampoline. With 2 dazzling routines, these sports stars will be judged on their technical prowess, execution, and the duration they spend soaring through the sky. In the end, only the gymnast with the highest total tally will be crowned champion in both sexes' events!

Next up, we have the fast and furious activity of handball! Teams of seven players each will battle it out on the court, passing and throwing the ball with lightning speed to score those crucial goals. With only 30 minutes per half, this intense sport demands precision and teamwork. The team with the most goals on the verge of the contest will triumph.

Also, be ready to witness the thrill of hockey, where players wield their sticks with precision to send the ball into the goal. With 11 players on each side, the field becomes a battleground of skill and strategy. Nail-biting matches played in four quarters of 15 minutes each will determine the champions

Next on the list is the martial art of Judo – an electrifying display of throws, pins, and submissions. On the tatami mat, athletes will strive for that decisive ippon to claim victory. With 15 events for both sex and a mixed-squad tournament, the judo matches will be a showcase of skill, technique, and determination!

Ah, now it's time to hit the water in the enthralling sport of rowing! Boats gliding gracefully on the water, propelled by synchronized oar strokes, will compete for glory on the 2000-meter course. With 14 events for men and women, rowing will showcase the perfect harmony of teamwork and athleticism!

Get ready for an exhilarating ride if you're a fan of rugby sevens! This fast-paced sport features seven players per team who will showcase their speed, strength, and agility as they sprint, tackle, and pass the ball with determination to score points. The matches consist of two halves lasting seven minutes each, guaranteeing non-stop action. At the end of the competition, the squad that accumulates the most points will emerge victorious in the tournament.

In addition, I highly recommend embracing the unpredictable winds by watching sailing competitions. With boats adorned with billowing sails gracefully gliding over open waters, competitors across various classes and games will battle it out. Sailors will navigate their way toward buoys marking the finish line to secure their positions on the podium.

Featuring 10 games for both sex, including a thrilling mixed event, sailing promises to captivate spectators with its nautical skill and strategic displays!

Let's not forget the precision and focus of shooting. Athletes will wield firearms or airguns, aiming at targets with pinpoint accuracy. From rifles to pistols and shotguns, they'll fire rounds at fixed or moving targets from various distances and positions. The shooter with the keenest eye and the highest score will reign victorious in the 15 gripping events of shooting – six for rifle, six for pistol, and three for shotgun.

Table tennis is a highly dynamic sport, with players showcasing lightning-fast agility. Picture the fast-paced action of paddles and balls flying across the table as competitors fiercely battle it out in both singles and doubles matches. With seven games in each match, players will constantly strive to reach that coveted 11-point mark. The upcoming Paris 2024 Olympics will feature five thrilling events in table tennis – men's singles, women's singles, men's doubles, women's doubles, and mixed doubles.

Get ready for the explosive power of taekwondo! This traditional Korean martial art is an exhilarating display of high-flying action, where athletes score points by executing precise and forceful kicks and punches. In thrilling matches that consist of up to three rounds, these talented warriors will compete fiercely for victory across eight taekwondo events – four for men and four for women.

Prepare to challenge yourself with the ultimate test of endurance – the triathlon! Athletes will face a rigorous 1.5-kilometer swim, a 40-kilometer bike ride, and a 10-kilometer run without any breaks. The individual or team with the fastest overall time will emerge victorious in the exhilarating men's individual, women's individual, and mixed relay events.

For volleyball enthusiasts seeking high-flying action, get ready to be captivated! Teams of six players will ignite the court as they spike and serve their way to triumph. With five sets per match and a tie-breaker if necessary, the excitement is guaranteed. The Paris 2024 Olympics will feature two volleyball events – the men's tournament and the women's tournament.

Diving is a sport that exudes elegance and grace. Athletes showcase their skills by leaping from platforms and springboards, executing impressive acrobatics in mid-air before smoothly entering the water. With four exhibitions for both sex, precision, and poise are paramount as divers compete for the greatest scores.

For those seeking a more challenging endeavor, marathon swimming awaits in the open waters. Brave swimmers take on the task of covering long distances in lakes, rivers, or oceans. The 10-kilometer course, marked by buoys and boats, sets the stage for an intense competition where the first swimmer to touch the finish line emerges as the champion.

Alternatively, you can immerse yourself in Artistic Swimming. It is a mesmerizing artistry (formerly synchronized swimming). Swimmers create stunning routines synchronized to music, seamlessly blending swimming, dance, and gymnastics. In perfect harmony, duet and team competitions showcase precision, synchronization, difficulty, and execution. Paris 2024 will showcase three captivating events: duet technical routine, duet free routine, and team free routine.

Then, we have the classic and dynamic sport of Swimming. Athletes will glide through the water using various strokes – freestyle, backstroke, breaststroke, and butterfly. In individual or relay races, swimmers will compete to touch the wall first and claim victory. With a whopping 35 events – 17 for men, 17 for women, and one mixed event – prepare for an aquatic spectacle like no other!

Now, brace yourself for the intensity of Water Polo! Teams of seven players each will pass, shoot, and defend to score goals in a rectangular pool. With four quarters of eight minutes each, the team with the most goals at the end of the game will triumph. If the score is tied, extra time and penalty shootouts will decide the winner. Water polo will feature two events – men's tournament and women's tournament.

Next, witness the raw power and strength of Weightlifting! Athletes will lift heavy barbells in two types of lifts – snatch and clean and jerk. Competing in individual events and divided into weight classes, weightlifters will strive to lift the most weight overall. Get ready for 10 events – five for men and five for women – showcasing incredible feats of strength.

And now, let's grapple with the sport of Wrestling! Wrestlers will use various techniques to grapple and pin their opponents to the mat or score points. In two styles – freestyle and Greco-Roman – wrestlers will compete in individual matches, aiming for falls or technical superiority. With 18 events in total – six for freestyle men, six for freestyle women, and six for Greco-Roman men – prepare for a display of athleticism and determination.

Also, get ready to groove with the newest addition to the Olympic family – Breaking! This dance sport, also known as breakdancing, will dazzle audiences as breakers showcase their acrobatic moves and footwork to music. In individual competitions, breakers will be judged on creativity, personality, technique, variety, performativity, and musicality. In Paris 2024, two events will feature the world's best breakers – men's breaking and women's breaking.

Sport climbing will once again captivate audiences with its three disciplines – speed, bouldering, and lead. Climbers will showcase their agility and strength as they race against time and gravity, aiming to reach new heights and conquer challenging walls. In Paris 2024, four events will be featured, including men's combined, women's combined, men's speed, and women's speed.

Skateboarding, which made its Olympic debut in Tokyo 2020, will return to Paris in 2024 with its two exciting disciplines – park and street. Skaters will showcase their creativity and style as they perform tricks and stunts on specially designed courses. With competitions for men's parks, women's parks, men's streets, and women's streets, skateboarding promises to bring the vibrant energy of youth culture to the Olympic stage.

Surfing, another relatively new addition to the Olympics, will make a splash in Paris in 2024 with its breathtaking performances on natural or artificial waves. Surfers will display their artistry and skills as they ride the waves, capturing the essence of the sport's connection with nature and the sea. Paris 2024 will feature two events – men's shortboard and women's shortboard – allowing surfers to showcase their talent and passion for the sport.

With such a diverse and dynamic array of sports on display, the Olympic Games Paris 2024 will provide an unforgettable experience for athletes, spectators, and fans worldwide. It will be a celebration of human potential, unity, and the enduring spirit of sportsmanship that transcends borders and cultures.

As the world gathers to witness the Olympic Games, we can look forward to witnessing extraordinary performances, inspiring stories, and the shared joy of competition, all in the spirit of friendship and fair play. Let the countdown to Paris 2024 begin!

CHAPTER 5

EXPLORING THE ICONIC LANDMARKS OF PARIS

Paris is an extraordinarily captivating city, comprised of a multitude of famous and remarkable landmarks that serve as testaments to its rich and fascinating history, culture, and aesthetic allure. Whether it be the extravagant Eiffel Tower, a structure that reaches great heights and serves as an emblem of Paris, or the esteemed Louvre Museum, which houses an array of invaluable artifacts, every corner of this enchanting city unveils a gem just waiting to be discovered. Accompany me on this exhilarating expedition as we delve deeper into some of the most renowned attractions that this captivating city has to offer.

Let us commence with an exploration of the ***Eiffel Tower***, an ultimate symbol of Paris.

Imagined and brought to life by the visionary Gustave Eiffel for the 1889 World's Fair, this iconic monument stands tall at an impressive height of 324 meters, attracting visitors from across the globe. Once you arrive, prepare yourself for a breathtaking experience as you witness the awe-inspiring panoramic views of Paris, unraveling before your very eyes from the tower's three elevated levels. It is not merely a tower; it is an all-encompassing encounter!

Envision relishing a delightful culinary experience at the tower's esteemed restaurant or indulging in a celebratory toast at the champagne bar, all while marveling at the city of lights below. Additionally, brace yourself for a thrill as you stand atop the glass floor, gazing down from above. To conclude your adventure, immerse yourself in the tower's museum, delving into its captivating history and heritage.

Now, let us discuss how you can reach this iconic destination. Fear not, intrepid explorers! You can conveniently secure your tickets online or at the ticket office upon your arrival. Numerous options are available for your perusal – ascend via the stairs or opt for the elevator to access the first or second level. Alternatively, indulge in the complete experience by riding the elevator to the summit! However, please be aware that ticket prices are subject to variation based on your age and the desired level you wish to ascend. Revered as a reliable resource, the official Eiffel Tower website offers comprehensive information regarding all pertinent details.

But dear readers, allow me to present the pinnacle of this excursion! To truly witness Paris in all its grandeur from the Eiffel Tower, one must ascend to the uppermost level, situated at a breathtaking height of 276 meters above ground level. From this vantage point, the view is nothing short of awe-inspiring, granting an unobstructed vision of the cityscape that surrounds you in all its glory. Gaze upon the array of iconic landmarks, including but not limited to the majestic Arc de Triomphe, the resplendent Louvre Museum, and the venerable Notre Dame Cathedral. You must seize the opportunity to utilize the telescopes and interactive screens, allowing you to zoom in and explore the enchanting nooks and crannies of the city that pique your curiosity the most.

However, the Eiffel Tower is not the sole vantage point available within the esteemed city of Paris. It behooves one to explore alternative locations, thereby allowing witnessing the resplendent tower from a fresh and invigorating perspective. Allow me to proffer a few recommendations for your esteemed consideration:

- In the initial phase, it is recommended to embark on a visit to the widely admired Place du Trocadéro, a prominent location strategically positioned on the opposite side of the winding Seine River.

By selecting this particular vantage point, one can take advantage of an ideal setting that enables the capture of exquisite photographs showcasing the magnificent Eiffel Tower in all of its grandeur. Furthermore, the observer is presented with a panoramic vista that encompasses the vibrant gardens and animated fountains below, thus provoking an irresistible sense of fascination.

- Another captivating option entails partaking in a stroll across the resplendent Pont de Bir-Hakeim, a bridge of monumental proportions that spans the graceful width of the Seine River. It is worth highlighting that this awe-inspiring structure provides an inimitable backdrop of steel columns and stately lanterns, ensuring that the beholder is presented with an awe-inspiring visual tableau. The resultant image firmly etches itself into the viewer's memory, creating an indelible impression that will not be easily forgotten.

- For those desiring a more grandiose experience, it would be prudent to venture forth to the magnificent Arc de Triomphe, an imposing edifice skillfully erected in honor of the towering achievements of the esteemed Emperor Napoleon Bonaparte. Upon ascending to the rooftop terrace, one is greeted with a truly awe-inspiring panorama that encompasses an unparalleled vista of the revered Eiffel Tower, as well as the storied expanse of the surrounding urban landscape. It is an encounter that shall elicit unmitigated admiration and leave an indelible mark upon the visitor's soul.

- To fully immerse oneself in the presence of the renowned Eiffel Tower, it is highly recommended that individuals make their way to the extensive and picturesque Champ de Mars – an extravagant park that gracefully stretches from the foundation of the magnificent tower to the distinguished École Militaire. Within this extraordinary sanctuary, one can indulge in periods of relaxation and pleasure, whether it be enjoying a delightful picnic on the luxuriant emerald fields or gazing upwards with boundless fascination at the breathtaking edifice majestically towering above. This exceptional encounter connects the observer to a profound feeling of astonishment and profound admiration.

- Finally, I would like to draw attention to the exceptional Hotel San Regis, which is highly regarded for its opulence and refinement. Within the prestigious confines of this establishment, one can indulge in an unparalleled luxury experience. The private balconies offer a breathtaking view of the iconic Eiffel Tower, adding to the enchantment. Additionally, patrons have the extraordinary opportunity to enjoy a romantic dinner in the esteemed restaurant, accompanied by the magnificent illuminated tower that graces the night sky, creating a truly captivating ambiance.

Now, let us delve into the topic of visiting the *Louvre* and immersing ourselves in the presence of its iconic masterpieces, including the world-famous Mona Lisa.

Prepare yourself for a mesmerizing journey through the expansive Louvre, a globally acclaimed museum renowned for its extensive collection of over 35,000 artworks from various civilizations and eras. From ancient Egypt to modern masterpieces, the Louvre showcases an awe-inspiring array of artistic treasures.

Here, you will encounter legendary creations such as the enigmatic Mona Lisa, the captivating Venus de Milo, and the triumphant Winged Victory of Samothrace.

Without any further delay, let us commence our monumental expedition to the illustrious Louvre! To acquire admission tickets, you have two convenient options: online booking or visiting the ticket office located on the premises. Alternatively, for a seamless and enhanced experience, the esteemed Paris Museum Pass or Paris City Pass is available, granting you the privilege of effortlessly bypassing queues. It is important to note that ticket prices may vary depending on age and preferred time slot. For comprehensive information, please refer to the official website of the Louvre.

To ensure an unforgettable encounter with the esteemed Mona Lisa and other exquisitely intricate masterpieces, allow me to share some invaluable recommendations:

- Carefully select the optimal timing for your visit: The Louvre is renowned for its bustling crowds, particularly during peak seasons and weekends. It would be prudent to exhibit astute judgment to navigate around the masses. Timely arrival in the early morning or late afternoon, alongside visits on Wednesday or Friday evenings, when the museum extends its operating hours until the splendid time of 9:45 p.m., will provide you with respite.

- Uncover concealed entrances: While the Pyramid entrance is widely acknowledged, it is no secret that it tends to attract a multitude of visitors. Instead, circumvent the queues by focusing on lesser-known entry points, such as the Carrousel du Louvre entrance, the Porte des Lions entrance, or the Richelieu entrance. This tactful maneuver will undoubtedly save you valuable time!

- Embrace the allure of guided tours: Given the vast expanse of the Louvre, navigating its labyrinthine corridors can indeed be overwhelming. Fear not!

Elevate your experience by embarking on an enthralling guided tour, which will steer you toward the crème de la crème of the museum, including the enigmatic smile of the Mona Lisa. Secure your tour in advance, either through the online platform or at the ticket office, and prepare for an enlightening artistic expedition.

However, that is not all! During your visit to the Louvre, please remember to practice patience and courtesy. Yes, the Mona Lisa may be an indisputable celebrity, attracting the attention of enthusiastic visitors. When you visit a museum, it's super important to show some respect and follow the rules they've set. That means no touching the artwork, putting away those selfie sticks, and no flash photography. But hey, don't worry! You'll have your chance to soak up all the beauty and awesomeness of those stunning masterpieces.

Now, let's switch gears a bit and take a look at the fascinating world of **Notre Dame**. This captivating cathedral is a true testament to the breathtaking Gothic architecture and the unbelievable skills of those stained glass artisans. It's like stepping into a magical realm!

Visualize the grandeur of Notre Dame, an iconic Parisian jewel, notable for its magnificent facade boasting three levels of majestic artistry. The lower level portrays captivating narratives from the lives of Christ, the Virgin Mary, and Saint Anne. Moving upward, the middle level features a splendid gallery of kings and a grand rose window, while the upper level is adorned with two majestic towers and a spire.

Ah, the towers! They soar to an impressive height of 69 meters, and for the adventurous souls willing to ascend 387 spiral steps, a reward awaits—chiming bells, grinning gargoyles, and a spellbinding panoramic view of Paris and its captivating landmarks.

Prepare to be captivated by the exquisite rose windows, those remarkable circular stained glass marvels that come to life as the sun graciously bestows its golden rays upon them. The cathedral boasts three of these breathtaking wonders—the west rose window on the facade, the north rose window on the left transept, and the south rose window on the right transept—each one a true masterpiece in its own right.

Now, let us delve into the captivating realm of flying buttresses—innovative arches that gracefully support the walls and roof of this majestic cathedral. They are not merely architectural marvels; they infuse the cathedral with a sense of dynamism and elegance, propelling it to the pinnacle of Gothic greatness.

Let me enlighten you on the matter of visiting the renowned Arc de Triomphe and taking a stroll along the illustrious Champs-Elysées.

painting a vivid picture of the awe-inspiring Arc de Triomphe— a colossal arch that boldly commands the heart of the bustling Place de l'Étoile, where countless avenues converge like the radiant rays of an ethereal star. In the year 1806, the ambitious Napoleon commissioned this monument to honor his mighty army and commemorate his triumphant victories This architectural marvel is adorned with intricate reliefs, captivating sculptures, and engraved inscriptions that vividly depict historical scenes, immersing the viewer in the captivating narrative of

French history. Moreover, it holds an even deeper significance as it is home to the sacred Tomb of the Unknown Soldier, accompanied by an eternal flame that serves as a powerful symbol of the bravery and sacrifices of those valiant souls who selflessly fought for France.

Are you prepared to embark upon your journey to witness this grand spectacle? Fear not, dear traveler! You may obtain your tickets in advance online or directly from the on-site ticket office. However, allow me to introduce a savvy approach to gaining entry—the Paris Museum Pass or the Paris City Pass grants you the delightful privilege of free access and the splendid opportunity to bypass the queue. Now, isn't that a delightful prospect? For detailed information regarding prices and availability, I recommend perusing the official Arc de Triomphe website.

However, before you fully immerse yourself in the grandeur of this architectural marvel, may I offer you some important advice? To reach this resplendent masterpiece, I highly recommend utilizing the subterranean passage that seamlessly leads you to the sidewalks of the renowned Avenue des Champs-Élysées. Please, I beseech you, refrain from venturing across the bustling street on the surface—an endeavor that may prove perilous due to the hustle and bustle of the traffic that surrounds you!

Once you find yourself within the arch, brace yourself for a delightful little adventure. Ascend the spiraling staircase comprising a total of 284 steps, and voila! You will be rewarded with a truly breathtaking view of Paris—an enchanting panorama that showcases the iconic Eiffel Tower, the artistic splendor of the Louvre

Museum, the majestic Notre Dame Cathedral, and a plethora of other magnificent sights!

But wait dear traveler—our excitement does not cease there! To continue your delightful escapade along the world-renowned Champs-Élysées, let us take a brief detour back through the underground passage to the opposite side of the avenue. I assure you, dear wanderer, a treat awaits you as you set foot upon one of the most sophisticated and esteemed boulevards in all of Paris—a splendid thoroughfare that stretches an impressive 1.9 kilometers, extending from the illustrious Place de la Concorde to the iconic Place de l'Étoile.

Allow yourself to be dazzled as you wander along this luxurious avenue, adorned with posh boutiques, charming cafes, exquisite restaurants, state-of-the-art cinemas, breathtaking theaters, and verdant gardens that infuse a touch of natural splendor within the urban tapestry. It is more than a mere street; it is a vibrant hub of celebration, where parades, festivals, protests, and ceremonies interweave to breathe life into this captivating avenue.

Oh, and do be sure not to overlook these hidden gems during your stroll:

1. The Grand Palais: Envision a colossal exhibition hall exuding sophistication with its stunning glass dome, majestic stone facade, and awe-inspiring metal structure. A testimony to the 1900 World's Fair, this cultural haven hosts captivating events, ranging from extraordinary exhibitions to soul-stirring concerts and everything in between.

2. The Petit Palais: As enchanting as its name implies, the Petit Palais is a smaller exhibition hall that also

emerged from the 1900 World's Fair. Its semi-circular shape and exquisite stone facade serve as a sophisticated abode for the City of Paris Museum of Fine Arts, wherein art enthusiasts like yourself may revel in masterpieces spanning various periods and artistic styles.

3. The Place de la Concorde: Experience the utmost magnificence as you step into the grandest square in the enchanting city of Paris. This historically significant site, once tainted by somber guillotine executions during the turbulent French Revolution, including the unfortunate demise of King Louis XVI and Queen Marie Antoinette, has undergone a remarkable transformation. It is now a picturesque wonderland adorned with exquisite fountains, majestic statues, and an ancient Egyptian obelisk, generously presented by the Khedive of Egypt in 1831.

4. The Arc de Triomphe du Carrousel: Prepare yourself for an unparalleled sight of pure grandeur, as a smaller yet equally awe-inspiring arch stands tall at the entrance of the legendary Tuileries Garden. Paying homage to the victorious triumph of the revered Napoleon at the historic Battle of Austerlitz, this remarkable arch draws inspiration from the prestigious Arch of Constantine in the eternal city of Rome. Boasting awe-inspiring sculptures and intricate reliefs that artfully narrate Napoleon's heroic campaigns, it is undoubtedly a spectacle to behold.

Therefore, my esteemed fellow explorers, let us don our comfortable footwear and embark upon an unprecedented journey through the wonders of the sublime Arc de Triomphe and the glorious Champs-Élysées. Here, an impeccable amalgamation of history, elegance, and beauty awaits, ensuring an indelible experience that shall forever remain etched within the depths of your heart.

But worry not, for the splendors of Paris extend beyond these magnificent landmarks. Allow me to guide you through the visitation of other illustrious attractions that grace the splendid city, including, but not limited to, the Sacré-Cœur, the Panthéon, and the Musée d'Orsay.

Firstly, the Sacré-Cœur shall captivate your senses with its unparalleled grandeur. Resting majestically upon the pinnacle of Montmartre Hill, this resplendent basilica is an architectural masterpiece, showcasing a harmonious fusion of Romanesque and Byzantine elements. Constructed between the years 1875 and 1914, the Sacré-Cœur mesmerizes with its striking white dome, a resplendent bronze Christ statue, and an enchanting mosaic depicting Christ in all His heavenly glory. Additionally, the breathtaking view from its terrace and dome shall leave you awe-inspired. Entry into the Sacré-Cœur is free, and for those seeking a moment of adventure, a small fee grants access to the dome. While in Montmartre, immerse yourself in the vibrant artsy atmosphere, exploring the charming Place du Tertre, the iconic Moulin Rouge, and the captivating Musée de Montmartre.

Secondly, we shall venture into the marvelous Panthéon, a resplendent mausoleum paying tribute to the luminous intellects of France. Originally conceived as a church, dedicated to the venerated Saint Genevieve, it transformed during the tumultuous French Revolution, becoming a secular temple of eternal remembrance. Prepare to be enthralled by its neoclassical facade, an architectural masterpiece, drawing inspiration from the grandeur of Rome's St. Peter's Basilica. Upon entrance, the crypt shall unveil the resting place of legendary figures such as Voltaire, Rousseau, Victor Hugo, Marie Curie, and many more. Access to this marvelous monument is granted through a fee or the utilization of esteemed passes such as the Paris Museum Pass or Paris City Pass.

Lastly, we shall indulge in the splendors of the Musée d'Orsay, a haven for connoisseurs of art. Housed within a resplendent former railway station, this transformed gem showcases a breathtaking collection of mesmerizing artworks from the 19th and early 20th centuries.

A marvel of architecture, its glass-roofed structure adorned with a unique clock tower surrounded by an intricate metal framework entices all who lay eyes upon it. Inside, one shall be enchanted by masterpieces from renowned movements such as Impressionism, Post-Impressionism, Art Nouveau, and Art Deco. Prepare to be captivated by the brilliance of creative geniuses such as Monet, Renoir, Van Gogh, Gauguin, Rodin, and countless others. Admission to this visual wonderland is obtained through the payment of a fee or by the utilization of esteemed passes such as the Paris Museum Pass or Paris City Pass, ensuring an unforgettable artistic experience.

To fully experience the wonders of Musée d'Orsay, I would like to take this opportunity to share some noteworthy highlights that will undoubtedly enhance your visit:

- Allow me to draw your attention to the magnificent clock tower, an iconic feature of Musée d'Orsay. Originally part of the esteemed railway station, this remarkable structure now offers a spellbinding panoramic view of the illustrious city of Paris. From here, you will have an unrivaled vantage point to appreciate renowned landmarks such as the Louvre Museum, Notre Dame Cathedral, and the awe-inspiring Sacré-Cœur. I encourage you to ascend to the fifth floor and immerse yourself in the beauty that lies before you.

- Prepare to be transported to a realm of vibrant colors, luminous light, and profound emotion as you step into the Hall of Mirrors.

This splendid exhibition space serves as a testament to the unrivaled brilliance of Impressionism and Post-Impressionism. Renowned artists such as Monet, Renoir, Degas, Cézanne, Van Gogh, Gauguin, and others have skillfully woven their magic onto the canvas, capturing exquisite scenes of nature, urban life, and the complexities of the human spirit. Prepare to be enthralled as you witness their artistry come to life.

- As you proceed, I implore you to explore the sculpture gallery, an expanse of grandeur that houses the most extraordinary sculptural creations of the 19th and early 20th centuries. Here, you will be captivated by the works of esteemed artists including Rodin, Carpeaux, Maillol, Bourdelle, and many others. Their evocative expressions, ethereal forms, and thought-provoking themes delve into the depths of human emotion, conveying tales of love, conflict, mythology, and historical events. Allow their masterpieces to resonate with your soul.

- Deeper within the museum lies a realm dedicated to the world of decorative arts, where you can truly immerse yourself in the awe-inspiring wonders of the 19th and early 20th centuries. The decorative arts gallery proudly showcases an array of exquisite furniture, ceramics, glassware, jewelry, textiles, and more. Each exquisite piece bears the indelible mark of the influential Art Nouveau and Art Deco movements, encapsulating the marriage of artistic brilliance and technical expertise. Prepare to be enthralled by the charm and craftsmanship that is on display before you.

CHAPTER 6

CULTURAL OFFERINGS
FOOD & ENTERTAINMENT

To truly capture the authentic essence of Paris, one is encouraged to wholeheartedly engage with its rich cultural heritage, diverse culinary delights, and vibrant nightlife. Within this chapter, I shall graciously impart a plethora of invaluable advice and refined recommendations, ensuring that you are fully equipped to partake in this captivating experience.

Acquiring Proficiency in Basic French Lexicon and Displaying Exemplary Etiquette

The acquisition of fundamental French phrases, as well as the embodiment of impeccable etiquette, represents an invaluable asset, facilitating an enhanced and harmonious encounter with the glorious city of Paris. Demonstrating a genuine effort to communicate in the native tongue garners genuine appreciation from the local populace, even if grammatical errors ensue. Please find below an overview of indispensable phrases and words deserving of your acquaintance:

- Bonjour (a cordial salutation)
- Merci (an expression of gratitude)
- S'il vous plaît (an enactment of politeness)
- Excusez-moi (a means to seek pardon)
- Parlez-vous anglais? (inquire about English proficiency)
- Où est...? (seek directions)
- Combien ça coûte? (discover the monetary value)
- L'addition, s'il vous plaît (request the bill)
- Au revoir (bid adieu)

In addition, please kindly observe the subsequent principles of decorum:

- Before requesting assistance or posing inquiries, cordially initiate the interaction with a bonjour or bonsoir (indicative of a delightful evening).

- Upon departing a retail establishment, restaurant, or similar establishment, kindly grace the host with expressions of gratitude, exemplified by merci and au revoir.

- Exercise discretion when utilizing tu (the informal form of address), instead, favor the employment of vous (the formal mode of address) unless an established familiarity exists.

- When acquainting oneself with a new counterpart, extend a handshake or proffer cheek kisses, the quantity of which is contingent on the existing level of intimacy.

- Exercise prudent judgment while compensating for services rendered, ensuring that the gratuity remains within the bounds of propriety. Often, a service charge is thoughtfully incorporated within the bill, nevertheless, if the quality of service warrants it, modestly supplementing with a few euros is considered quite acceptable.

- As a matter of refined conduct, abstain from consuming victuals or beverages whilst meandering public thoroughfares or utilizing public means of transportation. The indulgence in these activities is perceived as an affront to civility and social decorum.

- In spaces of cultural significance, such as museums, places of worship, and other hallowed establishments, kindly refrain from engaging in boisterous conversation or employing technological devices to ensure the preservation of tranquility and the atmosphere of reverence.

Guide to Experiencing the Finest French Epicurean Delights and Wines in the City of Light

Let us begin this tantalizing adventure with the iconic Croissant, a pastry so heavenly, it will transport you to a realm of pure bliss. With its delicate layers of flaky perfection and a rich infusion of butter, it is the epitome of indulgence. Whether it's a decadent breakfast or a delightful snack, this masterpiece can be found in every bakery and café, beckoning to be savored.

And what better companion to the Croissant than the legendary Baguette, a symbol of French culinary prowess? Its distinctive elongated shape, crowned with a crisp golden crust, encases a tender, pillowy interior that melts in your mouth. Whether enjoyed plain, with a touch of butter and jam, or adorned with the finest cheese and ham, this culinary marvel never fails to captivate.

Prepare your taste buds for the enchanting Crêpe, a delicate, thin pancake that dances on your palate with an array of delectable fillings. Sweet or savory, the choices are endless, allowing you to embark on a gastronomic adventure tailored to your desires. Tucked away in the nooks and crannies of popular tourist destinations, the aroma of these divine treats lures Parisians and visitors alike, offering a moment of pure joy.

- The Macaron: An intricately crafted cookie made from meringue and almond flour, adorned with a delightful core of sumptuous cream. These dainty confections are available in a stunning range of flavors and colors, waiting to be discovered and savored at renowned establishments such as Ladurée or Pierre Hermé.

- The Éclair: A slender pastry delight, bestowed with delectable custard filling and sumptuously coated with luxurious chocolate or other captivating glazes.

This culinary masterpiece can be relished in any Parisian bakery or pastry shop.

- The Quiche: A savory pie crafted with the finest eggs, cream, cheese, and an indulgence of delectable fillings, such as bacon, ham, spinach, or mushrooms. These gastronomic marvels can be discovered in delightful bakeries, charming cafés, and traditional brasseries.

- The Croque-monsieur: A grilled sandwich fashioned from freshly baked bread, harmoniously layered with succulent ham, tantalizing cheese, and a velvety béchamel sauce. This Parisian staple is available for indulgence in a variety of delightful cafés and brasseries, serving as an excellent option to satisfy midday cravings.

- The Croque-madame: A distinguished variation of the croque-monsieur adorned with a perfectly cooked egg, elevating this delectable creation to new heights.

- Ratatouille: A tantalizing vegetable stew beautifully composed of tomatoes, zucchini, eggplant, onions, garlic, and aromatic herbs. This enchanting dish can be relished at distinguished Parisian restaurants or cozy bistros, serving as either a delightful side or a satisfying main course.

- Boeuf bourguignon: A meticulously prepared beef stew, drenched and cooked to perfection in a rich red wine sauce, accompanied by luscious carrots, onions, mushrooms, and tantalizing bacon. This heartwarming dish is offered at esteemed restaurants and traditional bistros, providing a truly gratifying culinary experience.

- Coq au vin: A distinguished chicken dish marinated in red wine, paired with delightful mushrooms, onions, aromatic garlic, and a selection of fragrant herbs. This elegantly prepared entrée can be savored at renowned Parisian restaurants and charming bistros.

- Escargot: Succulent snails bathed in a tantalizing mix of flavorsome butter, garlic, and freshly chopped parsley. These exquisite delicacies can be enjoyed as appetizers at esteemed restaurants or traditional bistros.

- Foie gras: A culinary masterpiece of duck or goose liver, brought to its fullest potential through an exquisite force-feeding process. This sublime dish is savored as both an appetizer and a main course at refined restaurants and distinguished bistros.

- Soupe à l'oignon: How about treating your taste buds to a bowl of delicious onion soup generously topped with velvety melted cheese and served alongside some crispy, freshly toasted bread? This incredibly satisfying dish is a real crowd-pleaser and can be enjoyed as either a delightful appetizer or as a hearty main course at those iconic Parisian restaurants and cozy traditional bistros. So go ahead, and indulge in this ultimate comfort food!

- Salade niçoise: An exciting ensemble of lettuce, juicy tomatoes, succulent tuna, flavorful olives, boiled eggs, and anchovies, all beautifully adorned with a harmonious vinaigrette. This light and satisfying salad serve as a delightful main course or an exceptional accompaniment at refined restaurants and charming bistros.

- Crème brûlée: A heavenly custard dessert, crowned with a delicately caramelized sugar crust. This luscious treat awaits to be serenaded and savored at prestigious restaurants and inviting bistros, serving as the perfect conclusion to a remarkable meal.

- Tarte Tatin: An exquisite apple tart inverted in its preparation to showcase a delightful combination of caramelized sugar. This delectable dessert can be savored in various esteemed dining establishments, such as fine restaurants and charming bistros.

- Wine: France, the land of enchantment and passion, where every bottle tells a story and every sip ignites the soul. The artistry and dedication of French winemakers are unparalleled, as they pour their heart and soul into every drop, creating a tapestry of flavors that dance upon the tongue.

In the mesmerizing city of Paris, where love and beauty intertwine, the wine lover is greeted with an abundance of choices. From the humble wine shop to the grandest of eateries, a treasure trove of wines from diverse regions awaits, each one a testament to the rich tapestry of French viticulture. Let us embark on a sensory journey, uncovering the most renowned and coveted wines that embody the essence of French craftsmanship.

Champagne, the sparkling elixir that exudes elegance and celebration, hails from the illustrious Champagne region. Born from a harmonious blend of chardonnay, pinot noir, and Pinot Meunier grapes, this effervescent nectar graces the palate, adding an air of festivity and sophistication to any occasion. With each pop of the cork, joy is released, memories are made, and life becomes a shimmering celebration.

Bordeaux, a name whispered with reverence by wine connoisseurs around the world. From the revered vineyards of the Bordeaux region emerges a luscious red wine, crafted with meticulous care and composed of esteemed grape varieties such as cabernet sauvignon, merlot, cabernet franc, and other noble vines. A symphony of flavors dances on the tongue, as this full-bodied and complex nectar elevates every succulent bite of meat, transforming the dining experience into a divine revelation.

Burgundy, a region of endless allure and mystery, offers a tempting choice of either red or white wine. With a deft touch, winemakers skillfully craft these wines using the finest pinot noir or Chardonnay grapes. This elegant and fruity libation invites you to indulge in an enchanted rendezvous with the senses. It gracefully caresses the palate, enchanting with its exquisite flavors and captivating aromas, a harmonious dance of wine and cheese that leaves an indelible mark on the tapestry of memories.

Beaujolais, a hidden gem nestled in the picturesque Beaujolais region, unveils a delightful red wine crafted from the esteemed gamay grape. Like a gentle touch, this light and fruity elixir whisper secrets of the vine, pairing to perfection with delectable charcuterie or poultry dishes. With each sip, a symphony of flavors takes flight, a cascade of joy that tantalizes the taste buds and envelops the soul.

The enchanting Loire Valley, where a river of dreams winds through lush vineyards, gifts us with a refreshing choice of white or rosé wine. The Loire wines, ingeniously crafted from renowned grape varieties such as sauvignon blanc, Chenin blanc, cabernet franc, and other illustrious vines, are a breath of fresh air. With every sip, a crisp and invigorating nectar dances upon the palate, a refreshing companion to seafood or salad dishes. The senses are immersed in a delightful culinary experience, the symphony of flavors harmonizing like a choir of angels.

ASHLEY M. TUCK

How to discover the most exceptional dining establishments, captivating cafés, artisanal bakeries, and vibrant markets in the city of light

Parie, the eternal capital of gastronomy, boasts an extensive collection of dining options that cater to all tastes and preferences. From Michelin-starred establishments to charming street vendors, the city offers a cornucopia of culinary delights. To unearth the hidden gems amidst this culinary tapestry, one can rely on influential digital platforms such as TripAdvisor or Yelp, consult with knowledgeable locals for personalized recommendations, or simply rely on instinct and observation. Here are some valuable guidelines to assist in selecting the crème de la crème:

- Seek out establishments that exude a vibrant atmosphere without overwhelming crowds. This indicates their popularity while avoiding tourist traps.
- Pursue establishments presenting menus exclusively in French or with limited translations, as they faithfully cater to local discerning palates rather than tourists.

- Prioritize establishments offering daily specials or fixed menus, as these embody a commitment to utilizing fresh, seasonal ingredients while providing excellent value for money.

- Favor establishments displaying a certificate of excellence or adorned with the seal of prestigious guides such as Michelin or Gault & Millau. This signifies that these esteemed authorities have reviewed and bestowed their commendation upon these enterprises.

- Distinguish enterprises boasting the "fait maison" (homemade) or "produits frais" (fresh products) labels, showcasing their dedication to crafting their delicacy and utilizing top-notch ingredients of the utmost excellence.

A handful of the most captivating districts to embark on a quest for extraordinary culinary experiences, enticing cafés, masterful bakeries, and exciting markets in the city include:

- The Latin Quarter: Immerse yourself in the timeless charm of Paris's historic and student enclave, where a plethora of ancestral bistros, crêperies, brasseries, and enchanting cafés await. Noteworthy establishments include the iconic Shakespeare & Company bookstore and café.

- The Marais: Embark on a culinary voyage through the trendy heart of Paris, where an abundance of chic boutiques, art galleries, museums, and captivating cafés grace the streets. A visit to the famous L'As du Fallafel, a renowned falafel stand, comes highly recommended.

- Montmartre: Delight in the bohemian allure of Paris's artistic quarter, which reveals an array of cozy restaurants, artisanal bakeries, charming cafés, and inviting bars. Unmissable highlights include the iconic Sacré-Coeur basilica and the dazzling Moulin Rouge cabaret.

Have you ever heard of Saint-Germain-des-Prés? It's this amazing part of Paris that's just filled with intellect and a vibrant literary vibe. You're gonna love it! Picture refined and classy establishments all around, from fancy restaurants to charming cafés where you can sip on a coffee and soak in the atmosphere. And let's not forget about the bookstores and art galleries that make this place truly special. Oh, and you have to check out Café de Flore and Les Deux Magots - they're legendary! You won't find an experience quite like it anywhere else.

- The Champs-Élysées: Behold! The magnificent Champs-Élysées is a place distinguished by its allure and appeal to tourists far and wide. In this exalted sphere, an array of upscale restaurants, lavish shops, opulent cinemas, and vibrant nightclubs artfully coexist. Furthermore, one shall encounter the iconic Arc de Triomphe and the globally celebrated Eiffel

Tower, which grace this remarkable destination with their presence.

How to enjoy the nightlife and entertainment options

Whether you desire a night of dancing at a club, a theatrical performance, live music at a bar, or a romantic walk by the Seine, Paris offers something for everyone.

These are some of the top areas in Paris that are renowned for their vibrant nightlife and entertainment choices:

- Pigalle: Known as the red-light district, Pigalle features numerous cabarets, bars, clubs, and adult shops. The iconic Moulin Rouge can also be found here, offering spectacular shows featuring Cancan dancers and acrobats.
- Bastille: This lively and youthful neighborhood is home to a plethora of pubs, bars, clubs, and live music venues. The esteemed Opéra Bastille is also situated in this area, offering opera and ballet performances.

- Oberkampf: Considered the hip and alternative district of Paris, Oberkampf is a haven for trendy bars, clubs, and live music venues. The famous Nouveau Casino is located here, showcasing indie and electro bands.

- Montparnasse: A hub of cultural and artistic activity, Montparnasse is brimming with theaters, cinemas, and comedy clubs. La Coupole, a legendary brasserie frequented by icons like Picasso and Hemingway, can also be found here.

- Saint-Germain-des-Prés: Renowned for its sophistication and elegance, Saint-Germain-des-Prés boasts a selection of jazz clubs, piano bars, and cocktail lounges. L'Olympia, a famous venue that has hosted memorable concerts by renowned singers such as Edith Piaf and Charles Aznavour, is situated in this area.

To discover the best bars, clubs, pubs, and live music venues in Paris, there are several methods you can employ.

Online guides such as Time Out or Paris by Night offer valuable insights, seeking recommendations from locals can provide authentic suggestions, and following the crowd and the music can lead you to popular spots. Here are some tips to consider when choosing the ideal venues:

- Seek out establishments with happy hour or special offers, as they often provide discounts on drinks or food during specific times.
- Look for places that possess a distinct theme or style, aligning with your personal preferences or desired atmosphere.
- Prioritize locations with live DJs or bands, ensuring a captivating music and entertainment experience.

- Opt for venues with a reputable history and loyal clientele, as longevity and positive customer reviews signify quality establishments.

Here are a few of the best bars, clubs, pubs, and live music venues in Paris:

- Le Baron: A trendy and exclusive club that attracts celebrities and fashion-forward individuals. Entry may require being on the guest list or having connections.
- Le Batofar: Housed on a former lighthouse boat, Le Batofar has been transformed into a popular club and concert venue, offering electro music and live performances on its deck and interior.
- Le Caveau de la Huchette: A historic jazz club that has been hosting live music since 1946. Guests can enjoy swing music and dance in a unique vaulted cellar setting.

- Le Comptoir Général: A quirky and eclectic bar with a tropical theme, where patrons can indulge in exotic cocktails and enjoy African music in a jungle-inspired ambiance.

- Le Fumoir: A sophisticated and cozy bar, designed around a library theme. Here, guests can savor classic cocktails while sinking into leather sofas adorned with books.

CHAPTER 7

AVOIDING THE PITFALLS AND SCAM IN PARIS

Paris is a city renowned for its unparalleled beauty and captivating charm, yet it is not exempt from potential pitfalls and deceptive schemes. As a discerning visitor, it is imperative to remain cognizant of the latent risks and adversities that may present themselves in Paris, and learn how to mitigate or address them effectively. The ensuing chapter will provide invaluable guidance and counsel on how to ensure personal safety and optimal health, how to evade the nefarious attentions of pickpockets, panhandlers, fraudsters, and aggressive peddlers, how to respond to emergencies and accidents expeditiously, and how to address common quandaries and grievances encountered while traversing Paris.

Methods to Uphold Security and Well-Being in Paris:

Paris upholds a commendable reputation as a metropolis that is generally safe and salubrious.

However, it remains susceptible to acts of delinquency, acts of violence, and communicable ailments. To safeguard oneself and abide by principles of prudence, there are several measures one should undertake:

- Safeguard your valuable possessions by storing them securely or entrusting them to the confines of your lodging. It behooves you to avoid carrying copious amounts of cash or high-value items. If you do, ensure that they reside within a compartment that is both secure and close to your person.

- Exercise vigilance and circumspection concerning your immediate environment, avoiding dimly lit or isolated vicinities. Abstain from solitary nocturnal strolls or traversing unfamiliar neighborhoods unaccompanied. If circumstances elicit feelings of unease or apprehension, it is imperative to solicit assistance from local law enforcement or individuals amenable to aid.

- Refrain from accepting refreshments or sustenance from unfamiliar individuals, and diligently monitor your consumables to counteract potential tampering. Beware of substances such as drugs or toxins surreptitiously introduced into your provisions. Should symptoms of illness or dizziness arise, it is of paramount importance to summon medical assistance at the earliest convenience or consult a nearby pharmacy.

- Desist from indulging in tap water or the consumption of undercooked or raw comestibles, for they may harbor detrimental bacterial agents or parasites. Instead, embrace the consumption of bottled water or water that has undergone the process of boiling, as well as fully cooked or peeled edibles.

- Refrain from smoking or utilizing illicit substances in public locales, as such behaviors contravene the dictates of the law and incur the risk of prosecution or monetary penalties. Should the inclination to smoke arise, assiduously seek out designated areas or seek the necessary permissions.

- Only embark upon vehicular or bicyclic endeavors within Paris if one possesses a satisfactory degree of proficiency and self-assurance. Parisian roadways boast an environment of frenetic congestion and drivers epitomizing a predilection for assertive behavior. When navigating the cityscape, it is paramount to rely upon public transportation or licensed taxis.

- Ensuring the acquisition of travel insurance precedes one's sojourn in Paris is an unequivocal requirement. This indispensable safeguard serves to indemnify prospective medical expenses, reimburse for losses sustained due to theft or misplacement of belongings, or compensate for unexpectedly canceled flights. Exercise fastidiousness when perusing the intricacies of the policy, acquainting oneself with terms and conditions, and retaining readily accessible contact information about the insurer.

Tips for Avoiding Pickpockets, Beggars, Scammers, and Touts in Paris

Paris, being a highly sought-after tourist destination, unfortunately, attracts the attention of individuals engaging in unsavory activities such as pickpocketing, begging, scamming, and touting, all of which can be detrimental to unsuspecting visitors. These individuals employ a variety of cunning techniques designed to distract, deceive, or manipulate tourists into parting with their possessions or money. Maintaining a state of heightened awareness and familiarizing oneself with these common tactics is crucial to elude these individuals. Here are several noteworthy schemes to be mindful of:

- The Ring Scam: A perpetrator deliberately drops a ring close to you and subsequently feigns discovery. Attempting to either gift it to you or discern if it belongs to you, the individual will, upon your acceptance or contact, demand compensation for the item.

- The Petition Scam: A person wielding a clipboard will approach you, soliciting your signature for a purportedly commendable cause. However, the deceptive ploy surfaces as they proceed to coerce you into providing monetary contributions or divulging personal details. Do bear in mind that the petition itself is spurious, with funds directly benefiting the perpetrator.

- The Bracelet Scam: A perpetrator seizes the opportunity to affix a bracelet onto your wrist or finger, proclaiming it to be either a token of friendship or an earnest gift. Subsequently, they will implore you for monetary reimbursement or contributions to their charitable concerns.

- The Flower Scam: Individuals extend you a flower as an apparent act of virulent adoration or benevolence. Regrettably, their motives quickly manifest as they demand payment for the gesture, or implore you to contribute to their charitable cause.

- The Art Scam: Locals may approach you with an ostensible display of their artistic creations, asserting their sole proprietorship over the artwork. However, be cautious, as these individuals will subsequently press for monetary exchange, citing funding for their respective art schools or personal endeavors.

- The Taxi Scam: Dishonest taxi drivers may surreptitiously overcharge you or deliberately follow a lengthier route than necessary. This is often accompanied by claims of malfunctioning meters or a lack of change.

- The Ticket Scam: Perpetrators will attempt to sell counterfeit tickets for various museums, attractions, or events, occasionally asserting possession of additional tickets they have no use for.

- The Tout Scam: Visiting tourists may fall prey to individuals who offer guidance to purportedly superior or economically beneficial restaurants, hotels, shops, or attractions. These individuals will subsequently request payment either for their service or as commission from establishments they target.

To effectively avert such scams, it is essential that you:

- Exercise discretion in disregarding individuals who approach on-street asserting overly advantageous offers or requests.

- Refrain from accepting any offerings from unfamiliar persons, as well as limiting physical contact with both yourself and your belongings.

- Exercise vigilance when presented with documents for signature, thoroughly reviewing them before parting with personal information.

- Prioritize verifying prices and acquiring receipts before making any monetary transactions.

- Exercise caution when considering purchases from unauthorized vendors or suspicious sources.

- Never blindly follow individuals claiming to be guides or friendly acquaintances without first verifying their credentials or requesting references.

Guidelines for Managing Emergencies and Incidents in Paris

Paris, known for its secure and highly developed environment, nevertheless, acknowledges that emergencies and incidents can unfold indiscriminately and necessitates immediate attention. When confronted with any such untoward event in Paris, it is essential to understand the appropriate course of action and engage the appropriate authorities for assistance. Presented below are some of the prevailing circumstances and the recommended steps to address them effectively:

- In the event of sustaining injuries or illness, promptly contact 15 for immediate ambulance service or proceed to the nearest hospital or pharmacy. Alternatively, you may reach out to 112, the dedicated

European emergency hotline, or 18 to contact the fire brigade.

- If you find yourself victimized or as a witness to a criminal act, dial 17 to reach the competent police authorities or visit the closest police station. Moreover, 112, the European emergency hotline, and 114, exclusively catered to individuals who are deaf or hard of hearing, can also be contacted.

- In the unfortunate circumstance of misplacing your passport or other crucial documents, it is of utmost importance to promptly notify your respective embassy or consulate. These establishments meticulously handle cases of document replacement or issuance of temporary travel documentation.

- In the event of losing valuable items, such as credit cards, it is imperative that you expeditiously contact your bank or relevant service provider. They possess the necessary knowledge and expertise to assist you in canceling your card or recuperating your lost belongings.

- Should any accommodation, transportation, or service-related concerns arise, it is recommended that you directly contact the relevant entities and endeavor to find an amicable resolution. In cases where a satisfactory resolution proves elusive, seeking advice or assistance from a consumer association or a tourist office is highly advisable.

Strategies for Resolving Common Issues and Grievances in Paris

While staying in Paris, it is plausible that you may encounter certain predicaments or grievances, such as encounters with impolite service, language barriers, cultural disparities, or misunderstandings. To effectively navigate through these challenging situations, it is crucial to maintain patience, demonstrate politeness, and possess effective communication and negotiation skills. Presented below are some helpful tips for successfully handling such predicaments:

- Exhibiting respect and courtesy towards every individual you encounter in Paris is of paramount importance. Employing common greetings including bonjour, merci, s'il vous plaît, and au revoir, when engaging in conversation, expressing gratitude, making requests, or concluding interactions, fosters a culture of positive social exchange.

- Demonstrating flexibility and adaptability to local customs and practices in Paris is pivotal. Displaying an understanding that variances exist between your home country and France is essential in fostering a spirit of open-mindedness. Endeavoring to familiarize oneself with the cultural and etiquette norms prevalent in France can prove beneficial.

- Employing clear and concise language to express your requirements or preferences in Paris is pivotal. Simple words and gestures can be employed if proficiency in the French language is limited. Avoid making assumptions that English is universally spoken or that your accent is readily comprehensible.

- Maintaining composure and assertiveness when confronted with issues or grievances in Paris is crucial. Avoid resorting to a raised voice or tempestuous conduct. Concisely articulate the situation at hand and your desired outcome, employing politeness coupled with firmness. Do not hesitate to request the attention of a manager or supervisor, if required.

- Adhering to reasonableness and realism whilst seeking remedies or compensation in Paris is vitally important. Strive to maintain equilibrium and embrace a fair resolution. Abstain from exhibiting greed or engaging in disingenuous behavior.

By adhering to these guidelines, one is equipped to circumvent the majority of pitfalls and potential scams in Paris, ensuring the seamless handling of emergencies, incidents, challenges, and grievances that may arise. Consequently, one can wholeheartedly embrace and enjoy Parisian culture, cuisine, and nightlife devoid of any apprehension or remorse.

THE END

Dear reader,

I extend my heartfelt gratitude for acquiring a copy of this work. Your decision to embrace it fills me with immense joy, knowing that I have been able to offer assistance through my words.

In the spirit of sharing joy, I kindly request you to consider leaving a review and spreading the word among others. Your support holds significant meaning to me.

If, by any chance, this piece did not meet your expectations, please accept my sincere apologies.

I assure you that I am committed to improving and striving for excellence in future endeavors. However, above all else, please remember that your act of acquiring this copy demonstrates that you are cherished and loved.

Once again, thank you for your support and for being a part of this journey.

Warm regards,
[Ashley M. Tuck]

ASHLEY M. TUCK

Made in the USA
Las Vegas, NV
02 December 2023

81966807R00095